Blockchain in Business

by

Colin Holiday

Table of Contents

Legal Notes	5
Introduction	6
Section 1: The Basics of Blockchain	8
Chapter 1. Understanding Blockchain	9
In Blockchain we Trust	9
What is Blockchain?	10
The Importance of Blockchain	11
Chapter 2. How Does Blockchain Work?	13
Traits of a Blockchain ledger	13
Centralized vs. Decentralized	14
Components of a Blockchain ledger	15
The 3 Principles of Blockchain	15
How a Blockchain is Created	17
Blockchain Protocols	18
Chapter 3: The Mining Process	20
Hashing	20
Proof of Work	22
Proof of Stake	23
How Long it Takes to Create a Block	23
Changing Transactions After They Are Added to a Block	23
Invalid Transactions and the Blockchain	24
51% Attack	25
Chapter 4: Bitcoin and Blockchain	27
The Increasing Difficulty of Bitcoin Mining	28
The Bitcoin Mining Process	29

Cloud Mining	30
Mining Pools	30
Section 2: From Concept to Reality	**31**
Chapter 5: Blockchain Applications	**32**
Sidechains	32
Blockchain in Business	34
Considerations when Implementing Blockchain	36
Chapter 6: Challenges of Implementation	**38**
Technical Challenges	38
Business Challenges	39
Regulation Challenges	41
Chapter 7: Using Blockchain Technology	**43**
Blockchain Use in Monetary Administration	43
Blockchain Use in Property Transactions	44
Other Uses of Blockchain	45
Chapter 8: Real World Examples	**47**
Blockchain Consortiums	47
Other Real World Examples of Blockchain in Business	50
Conclusion	**54**

Legal Notes

Copyright 2018 - All rights reserved

This document contains opinions and ideas of the author. It is sold for the purpose of providing helpful and reliable information; the publisher, author, and all other parties involved in the making of this document are not required to render any qualified services or advice.

The information provided herein is strictly for educational purposes; any liability, in terms of inattention or otherwise, by any usage or abuse of any policies, processes, or directions contained within, is the solitary and utter responsibility of the reader.

Under no circumstances will any legal responsibility or blame be held against the publisher, author, or any other parties involved in the making of this document for any reparation, damages, or monetary loss due to the information herein, either directly or indirectly.

Permission is not granted to reproduce, duplicate, or transmit any part of this document in electronic or printed format. Recording of this publication is also prohibited and storage of this document is not allowed without the written permission from the publisher. All rights are reserved.

Introduction

Over the past couple of decades, the internet has grown bigger and closer to individual households and organizations, this has caused disruption in a number of industries from retail, to telecommunications, to transportations. Of these industries, none have been turned upside down as much as the financial sector has been in recent times due to Blockchain technology.

Blockchain has changed the way people deal with their finances due to the efficiency and security it provides; a number of institutions are implementing Blockchain in their processes in order to improve the functionality of their business.

Cryptocurrencies, such as Bitcoin and Etherium, have come about as a result of Blockchain. This meteoric rise in the price of Bitcoin has sparked a frenzy in cryptocurrency and its related markets with over a thousand different cryptocurrencies being traded on exchanges daily.

On the other side of the coin, Blockchain as a technology has sprouted a number of revolutionary ideas that are driving businesses. Many industries from healthcare, to banking, and even retail are adopting Blockchain in an effort to gain an edge over their competitors.

This book explains the basics of Blockchain and explores the challenges of Blockchain use in business. Divided into two sections, the first explains the history and the basic elements of Blockchain along with its original use in Bitcoin. The second section gives a look at the challenges and opportunities in implementing Blockchain in business today, as well as some examples of companies who have already successfully developed Blockchain into a business use to help you understand the possibilities that this new technology brings.

Please do note that ***this is NOT a technical book***. If you are looking for understanding on how to solve the cryptographic algorithms, want to learn about coding a block, or want to read up on cryptography, this book is not for you. Nevertheless I hope that you will enjoy learning about this exciting new technology and the opportunity it brings to us all.

Section 1: The Basics of Blockchain

Chapter 1. Understanding Blockchain

The Blockchain is an open, global, peer-to-peer platform that alters the fundamentals of what can be done online, as well as the manner in which we do it. This technology opens up new and novel ways of conducting business, if we were to open our minds to the possibilities. Blockchain itself brings a robust and different next-generation method to register and exchange tangible and intangible assets. As some experts have summarized it, the Blockchain is a digital medium for the exchange of value.

In Blockchain we Trust

Blockchain a technology that facilitates peer to peer transactions, this means that it removes the need for intermediaries by connecting parties directly. An example of this in the financial sector is the direct transfer of funds between parties without involving banks and financial institutions. However it does this in a manner that keeps the identities of both parties confidential, by validating the information against prior transactions and keeping a record of all the transactions.

This means that any personal information acquired is private and not transmitted to the other party. It is possible for the buyer and seller to conduct a trade and pay for goods and services without either party knowing the identity of the other. This is because the transaction is reconciled through mass collaboration and then encrypted and stored in a digital ledger.

The Blockchain system has the ability to hold documents ranging from title deeds, educational degree certificates, to legal contracts, or even personal identification. This is due to the fact that Blockchain permits smart contracts. This is a computer protocol intended to facilitate, verify, and enforce a contract digitally in a verifiable and irreversible manner.

What is Blockchain?

Blockchain was originally designed as an accounting framework for the cryptocurrency known as Bitcoin, which was supposed to address unified, controlled monetary standards that were subject to fluctuations in value. It was intended to be a digital currency that would avoid the fluctuations caused by real world market factors. The first Blockchain was therefore implemented by Bitcoin.

So how then does the Blockchain work? Using Bitcoin as an example, when we buy a product using cryptocurrency the Blockchain network creates a transaction. The funds are then transferred from a digital wallet, and confirmed by all the nodes (users) running the Blockchain. This is checked against the ledger in the Blockchain to ensure that there is sufficient funds to perform the transaction, and then it is added to the Blockchain as another transaction.

These transactions are recorded on the Blockchain using a hash function. This breaks down the transaction into a series of characters, which is performed by the software, creating a complex mathematical problem. This is then solved using sheer computing power, which may take trillions of attempts, and then verified by other peers. This solving of mathematical problems is known in the cryptocurrency world as "mining", as those that solve these problems are rewarded with an amount of cryptocurrency. The hashes that are solved are entered into the ledge of the Blockchain, and are then confirmed. For more information on mining, see Chapter 3.

This makes each transaction both secure and transparent as it can be seen by all nodes or users, preventing any possibility of fraud. This also keeps records private and safe, as the transactions are stored as encrypted blocks on the Blockchain.

The Importance of Blockchain

The Blockchain is essentially a decentralized online platform that deals with contracts. In terms of cryptocurrency, this refers to financial transactions, but it can be used for other contracts such as identity data, product or component history, or any type of data. What is important is the decentralization of the platform, which means that the data exists in more than one location.

The current online payment gateways such as PayPal and other eWallets are integrated with a bank account or credit card to send and receive money. Blockchain being decentralized exists as code across a network, which bypasses these middlemen such as PayPal, eWallets, or banks.

The main traits of the Blockchain are:

1. It keeps a record of all transactions.
2. It is able to establish contracts.
3. It is able to establish identities.

These three services explained above are usually performed by financial institutions and middle men, and the decentralization of these roles means that these middle men can be replaced by the Blockchain. With the huge market capital of the financial industry, replacing these roles with the Blockchain would have a great impact of disrupting the industry. It might even result in increased efficiency within the business if implemented correctly.

Outside the financial industry, the ability to establish contracts plays an important role as it keeps a record of an activity between two parties. Blockchain is able to store information digitally as encrypted codes. By entering a unique key, individuals are able to "sign in" and agree to or execute a contract.

Using this system, it is possible for "smart technology" to be used to connect objects with companies. Monitoring software could be used to control the access to items or locations, which can be useful in issuing electronic tickets to events or movies. The same technology could be used to keep records with certain devices and transmit them to authorities, such as in the use of equipment; these records can then be used for billing purposes or to monitor the condition of equipment for servicing. Because of the fraud proof capability of Blockchain, it is able to be put into use in many different aspects in a myriad of industries as we will explore in Chapter 7, and Chapter 8 will provide some real world examples of these applications.

Chapter 2. How Does Blockchain Work?

A ledger is a record or database containing the entirety of accounts relating to transactions of an organization's financial information. Traditionally ledgers are used in accounting to record assets, liabilities, owner's equity, revenue, and costs.

Traits of a Blockchain ledger

The Blockchain is a ledger or record of transactions, shared across multiple computers. Because Blockchain can be used in the context of many different types of operations, we need to identify a list of characteristics that define and differentiate Blockchain ledgers from the rest.

Blockchain transactions:
- Are recorded on multiple nodes
- Takes place on a peer-to-peer (P2P) network
- Are created and accessed by peers
- Are encrypted
- Uses a digital signature to verify identities

The above list of features is what differentiates a Blockchain from a regular database. Most notably, new entries are distributed to other notes in the network which updates the database universally. These updates are done through the network and comply with the agreed upon requirements.

Centralized vs. Decentralized

Centralized Ledgers

Centralized platforms requires all data to pass through a single point or node. Every transaction will have to be communicated to a main server or hub, where information is stored.

Because all data is stored on a single node, if a node is taken offline it will affect the access to the system. Being limited to a single note also makes the ledger susceptible to hacking or cyber attacks.

Decentralized Ledgers

Decentralized ledgers are connected through multiple points, and the data is stored on multiple nodes. Decentralized platforms are also known as "peer-to-peer networks". An example of a decentralized network are BitTorrents where there are multiple seed files and downloads happen concurrently from multiple sources.

Decentralized ledgers work on the same peer-to-peer principle, storing the ledger in multiple nodes. In this way, if a single node is offline it is still possible to maintain the integrity of the ledger making it less prone to attacks.

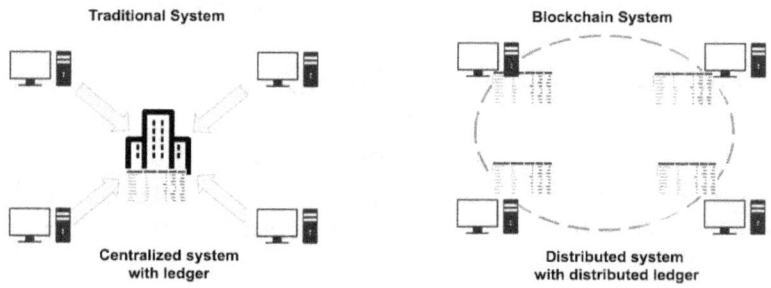

Image 01: Centralized vs. Decentralized Networks.

Components of a Blockchain ledger

There are three essential components to understanding how Blockchains are made.

1. A system of networked computers
2. The protocol that the system operates on
3. A process for the nodes of the network to offer consensus

The term "Blockchain" in fact, describes how transactions on the ledger are made. In reality, a Blockchain is simply data stored on a file similar to any other file on your computer, such as an image, a video, a document, or a program.

The 3 Principles of Blockchain

There are three main principles of a Blockchain, and while individually each of them are nothing new putting them together results in a revolutionary way of validating and executing peer-to-peer transactions.

The three main technologies of Blockchain are:

A Private Cryptographic Key

A private cryptographic key is a variable that is used with an algorithm to encrypt and decrypt codes. While the algorithm itself does not need to be kept secret, the key should be. This gives privacy and security to the person holding the key, and this is not even shared with the other party in the transaction.

Each Blockchain transaction generates a signature from the private key, and without the key it is impossible to make a fraudulent transaction.

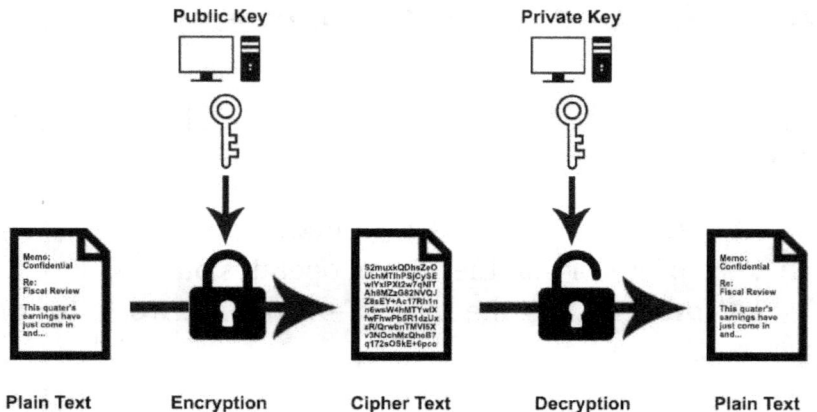

Image 02: How a private cryptographic key works.

A Decentralized Network with a Shared Ledger

The limitation of private and public keys is that they only authenticate a transaction. This does not secure digital relationships, which combines the keys and the transaction, thereby approving and legitimizing each transaction. Therefore a distributed ledger is used.

A distributed ledger is a database that is consensually shared and synchronized across network spread across multiple nodes. This keeps a copy of each and every transaction, making security breaches significantly more difficult. Also, since changes to any transactions are shared across the network this makes fraud easier to detect.

In the event that a system gets hacked and data is altered, the other nodes in the network are not very likely to get affected because of the distributed and decentralized nature of the network. Hacking such a network requires a huge amount of effort and innumerable resources, thus the larger the network is the more secure it will be.

An Incentive to Service the Network's Transactions

Since hashing (aka validating or "mining") transactions require a huge amount of computing power, electricity, and other costs there has to be an incentive for people to do this. In cryptocurrency it is common for miners to be awarded a small amount of cryptocurrencies for each successful block that is added to the Blockchain.

However, as the volume of contracts in a Blockchain increases, the difficulty of hashing also increases which affects the computing power required. In the case of Bitcoin, it is becoming more common for users to attach a transaction fee to a payment which is gradually replacing the reward per block hashed in the Blockchain.

How a Blockchain is Created

To be part of the Blockchain system, software needs to be installed by to connect a computer or server to the network thereby becoming a node in the network. Each node in the network manages a Blockchain which is in effect a database. Nodes act as entry points for new data and are responsible for checking and distributing new data that has been sent to the Blockchain.

These nodes act in concert to validate transaction data, and separately store the Blockchain. Each block will have a protocol that is a pre-agreed rule for technical and business validation of the data. This helps the entire network to reach a consensus on the data and validating each transaction as it is added to the Blockchain. These blocks are added in chronological order, in a way that it resembles a chain and hence the name Blockchain.

There is no central database or authority; if a person wants to claim they are the original owner of the block, it can be traced from the latest block of transactions all the way to the first block known as the "genesis block."

Blockchain Protocols

Every time a transaction is created, it becomes a block that is linked to the block that was created before it, thus forming a chain. Blocks are then grouped together into neighborhoods, determined by the algorithms of the system.

In the case of Bitcoin, it uses the Bitcoin Blockchain Protocol, which dictates that each transaction must be built upon the previous transaction to guarantee that it is legitimate. However, this protocol is not built into Blockchain itself, and different Blockchains may use different protocols.

As technology advances and Blockchain gains in popularity, new protocols that have better security, privacy, or are more efficient are being developed and applied to different uses. Some examples include the Ripple Transaction Protocol (RTXP), NEM, and Ethereum.

These protocols differ in improvements or variations to the different aspects of Blockchain, from Ethereum's transitioning from proof of work algorithms to proof of stake algorithms. Another example would be NEM Blockchain platform's use of their Proof of Importance algorithm, which focuses on smart assets and enterprise systems. NEM's Blockchain platform is completely API driven and easier to integrate with existing systems.

The concept of Blockchain is universally applied to each of these protocols, but with the features and emphasis tweaked each of these protocols have evolved differently to suit different needs, different industries, or to address different challenges. It is important when looking at Blockchain to understand that the protocols that drive the Blockchain, and how it presents unique opportunities and challenges.

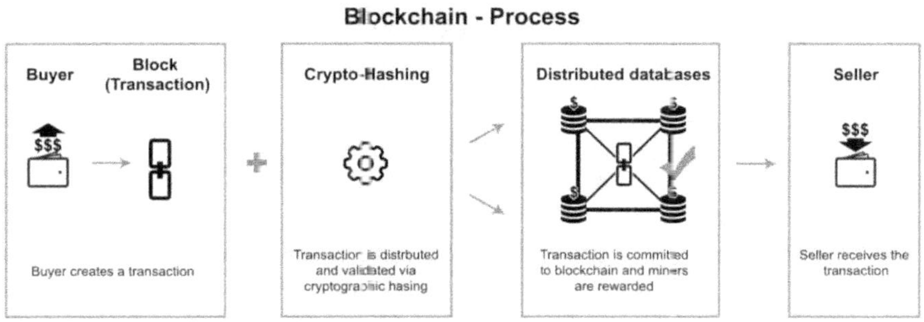

Image 03: The Blockchain process

Chapter 3: The Mining Process

The Blockchain relies on miners to process the blocks. Miners are the ones who validate transactions and build the blocks in the Blockchain. Computer processing power is used to solve cryptographic mathematical puzzles. This produces a "hash", which is unique to each set of transaction data.

Different algorithms will produce different hashes, and there are a number of different protocols that can be used to create a Blockchain. What is important is that the entire network of miners agree to the protocols and algorithms. For an example of mining, see the section in Chapter 5 on Bitcoin Mining.

Hashing

Blockchain transactions must be recorded in a specific ordered manner, and this protocol is determined by the hash. A hash is a function that is used to map data to a string of data of a smaller size.

The hash contains information about the order of the block, and information about the contents of the block. It reveals the block's number, the time and date of the block's registration, and the number of transaction that are contained within the block. The hash appears as an encrypted hexadecimal figure, and is also known as key.

Hashes are ideal, more so than timestamps or other forms of categorizing data. Hashes are generated by individual users using algorithms provided by specific software. When the hashes match the data, the mixtures will join the chain. Through this process, you can be sure that the string is internally consistent. Generating hashes is laborious and time-consuming. If you want to make retroactive changes to the data in the chain, then you would have to remake all the mixtures up to that point forward for them to be consistent. This means the Blockchain will appear very different.

While producing a hash from data like a transaction block is not difficult, it is impossible to work backwards to figure out the hashed data by viewing the hash. Each hash is unique even if the procedure to produce it is simple. Changing a single character in the data results in a completely different hash.

A hash is generated by formulating together, the transactions in a block with the hash of the last block stored in the Blockchain. This process enables the hash to act like a digital wax seal that confirms the chronology of every block in the chain and ensures that any tampering would be visible to every entity present. This, the Dominoes effect is in effect in the Blockchain, since any tampered hash would result in the hash of the next block is wrong, which will continue throughout the chain.

It is important to note that a hash created by an algorithm will always be the same for the same string of input. Changing, adding, or removing a single character in the input will result in a totally different hash result.

Each block contains a few essential elements:

- The hash of the block before it,
- A list of transactions to be added,
- A (guessed) number solving the puzzle, and
- A timestamp and ancillary information

After compiling the necessary elements of a block, the miner begins the process of hashing. Since a small change to the input will result in substantial changes to the hash, a single value is changed with each interaction, this value called the nonce. The process is continually repeated until the cryptographic puzzle is solved.

Due to the complexity of the hash as explained above, the main way that is used to solve these cryptographic puzzles is through brute force. Miners guess at the answers, and rely on having a large amount of computer processing power to generate guesses at an incredible rate which can go into the billions, trillions, or even quadrillion hashes per second.

Proof of Work

Miners that solve the cryptographic mathematical puzzles and add valid blocks to the Blockchain are rewarded for contributing computer power. The block that they add to the Blockchain is known as proof of work.

In order for the proof of work to be added to the Blockchain, it has to be verified by the other miners. Once a solution to the puzzle is found, the other miners are then tasked to
verify the answer with the solution described.

By solving this puzzle, it acts as proof that computing power, electricity, time and resources were contributed to the network. A reward is commonly given to the miner that solves the puzzle as compensation for the cost of adding the block to the Blockchain.

Proof of Stake

An alternative algorithm to verify the authenticity of transactions in a block is the Proof of Stake model which tries to achieve a distributed consensus. Instead of having miners compete to solve a puzzle and then award coins to the one that solves it like in the Proof of Work model, in the Proof of Stake model the miners instead are rewarded for their effort with transaction fees.

This allows blocks to be chosen by random selection, usually based upon its wealth or value.

How Long it Takes to Create a Block

Blocks are discovered randomly through a process, therefore it is not possible to tell how long it will take for a certain number of blocks to be chained. However it is popularly believed that it takes an hour to build a community standard of six blocks, as it takes on average 10 minutes to find each block.

The difficulty of mining increases with the size of the blocks as larger blocks will contain a longer chain. The processing speed of the nodes in the network however, will also play a determining role. With improvements in processing power and computer technology, the time to form a block will be reduced as well.

Changing Transactions After They Are Added to a Block

Transactions added to a block, it is more or less permanent. Any attempts to create a fake transaction or alter a transaction by changing a block that has already been stored in the Blockchain, will not work since that block's hash would totally change. Since each block makes references to the previous block, it is impossible to change a single transaction in the Blockchain without altering the entire chain itself.

If the block's authenticity is checked by a miner with the help of the hash function, the hash would be different from the one already stored alongside that block in the Blockchain. Any attempts at fraud will be revealed at this point.

Aside from the near impossibility of the task, this is also an extremely time consuming process that requires a large amount of processing power. The difficulty and complexity of this is further increased as the number of transactions in the Blockchain grows, making the hash longer and longer over time.

It is estimated by Bitcoin that after six blocks are added on top of a block, it is impossible to change any transactions in that "neighborhood". The number of blocks on top of a transaction is sometimes also be referred to as confirmations; there are some organizations that will wait for six confirmations before accepting a payment as assurance the operation will not be changed on the Blockchain.

Invalid Transactions and the Blockchain

Every time a transaction occurs, it creates a pending transaction which must be validated. This transaction is then sent to everyone on the network, and it is validated and added to the Blockchain. The person that groups it with other pending transactions and adds a valid block of operations to the Blockchain gets a reward as explained earlier.

Since everybody in the network can see who who has performed a transaction and the details of each transaction. As everyone is aware of the transactions that occurred before, they will be also be aware when someone tries to spend currency above a value that they own.

However, there are issues when miners do not fully validate a block before mining on top of it. As validating a block takes time, this may be done in the interest of saving time and improving the efficiency of mining. However, once a block is recognized as invalid the entire block is thrown out.

51% Attack

A 51% attack, also known as a majority attack, is a hypothetical attack on a Blockchain. Hypothetical as such an attack has yet to occur, although it has come close to occurring in the past.

When a group of miners control more than half of a network's mining hash rate, it is possible for this group to disrupt the validity of transactions. Whether this is done by reversing transactions, invalidating payments, or causing all sorts of interference.

This group can prevent miners from completing blocks, monopolizing the rewards, or block the transactions from certain users altogether. After all, by controlling the majority of the hash rate they have significant influence of what goes into the block chain. Note that it is only likely that a group with 51% can control the Blockchain; it is not a 100% guarantee.

At the current scale of mining, a 51% attack is unlikely as even a large-scale government organization may not have sufficient resources to pull it off. If someone controls 51% of the hash rate, it is possible for the person to reverse transaction that he has made, or prevent transactions and blocks from forming. Such an attack would enable the person who controls 51% of the mining hash rate to keep all the coins for himself.

Chapter 4: Bitcoin and Blockchain

To further understand Blockchain, it is important to understand Bitcoin. Bitcoin is an electronic currency, started in late 2008. It was originally intended as a peer-to-peer electronic virtual currency system, allowing individuals to buy, sell, trade, and hold them as assets. As each transaction does not require a bank or financial institution to authenticate, any Bitcoin transaction is intended to be almost instantaneous, and are secured after an hour from submission.

The main use of Bitcoin is for peer-to-peer transactions, serving as a medium of exchange similar to any other currency like US Dollars, British Pounds, Euros, or Japanese Yen. You can exchange these currencies for good or services, like a meal at a restaurant, or clothes at a shop. Similarly, Bitcoin can serve the same purpose.

As with any brick-and-mortar cash transaction, there is no record of which individual gave which dollar bill. Although a transaction is known to have taken place, it does not pass through a bank or financial institution since there is an establishment of trust in the business, and in the currency. The proof of work in the currency of Bitcoin allows trust to carry out the transaction, and a third party financial institution is not needed.

The value of Bitcoin comes from the trust that exists between peers that participate in the market as it is not regulated by banks or governments; proof of work in the above example is sacrosanct to the value of the currency, as it ensures that the buyer has sufficient funds for the transaction, and the seller is receiving the correct amount for the sale. In this way, it is a currency or cash asset.

As proof of this, a number of businesses are already accepting Bitcoin as of the writing of this book. One example is Expedia, which has allowed users to pay for hotel bookings since June 2014. Microsoft also allows Bitcoins to be used, depositing them into your Microsoft account allows you to buy games, movies and other apps in the Windows and Xbox stores. Additionally, a number of businesses are accepting Bitcoins in their stores worldwide.

The Increasing Difficulty of Bitcoin Mining

There are only 21 million Bitcoins available, and as more and more Bitcoins are cirulated, the longer it takes to mine one. Because of this, the more Bitcoins there are in the market, the harder it is to mine Bitcoins. It is estimated that it takes ten minutes on average to solve a block containing the latest transaction data by miners, with the help of cryptographic hash functions

Bitcoins are rewarded to miners when they validate transactions, and the network compensates them with digital coins for contributing with the necessary computational power to provide a proof of work. Naturally the reward is directly proportional to the computing power a person contributes to solving the hashes. The more processing power you put in, the more coins you get for solving hashes.

This requires special programs and high-end computers, usually costing in the thousands of dollars in order to get the most efficiency. However, with the difficulty of hashing rapidly increasing, competition is high and as a result the rewards are being claimed by the miners that are able to scale and solve the complex mathematical problems quickly and cheaply.

Also, the Bitcoin network is designed to produce a constant amount of Bitcoins every 10 minutes. With an increase in miners, the mathematical algorithms that are generated has to increase in order to adjust to the increase in the hash rate of the network. This artificially throttles the production of Bitcoins, making it harder to actually mine Bitcoins profitably.

The Bitcoin Mining Process

This is the mining process for Bitcoins:

Step 1: Every ten minutes pending Bitcoin transactions (a "block") is collected by miners and turned into a mathematical puzzle via algorithms.

Step 2: The miners try to solve the puzzle by guessing at random. Due to the hash function, it is impossible to predict the outcome as changing a single number or character will result in a vastly different hash. Therefore using a brute force technique and applying the has function will eventually lead to the solution.

Step 3: The first miner to find the solution announces it to others on the network. The rest of the miners immediately switch over to validating the solution and the transaction. They check the answer to the mathematical puzzle, as well as ensure that the sender has sufficient funds to send over for the transaction.

Step 4: If there is a consensus that the solution is correct, the block is cryptographically added to the ledger and the miners move on to the next block of transactions.

Cloud Mining

As mining becomes more and more resource intensive, cloud mining has appeared recently to allow miners to mine cryptocurrency without managing the hardware. Instead, miners purchase "mining contracts", which enables them to buy the output of Bitcoins mined from the hardware during the term of their contract.

For example, if a miner were to purchase a mining contract for a day then whatever amount of Bitcoins mined from the cloud mining service in that day would belong to the miner.

Mining Pools

Mining pools are another way that miners are getting around the escalation of computing power required to mine cryptocurrencies like Bitcoin. This is done by combining the computing power of several miners; this method has gain in popularity as the difficulty of mining has increased to the point where it would take a huge amount of time to generate blocks. The rewards for mining pools are usually distributed according to the amount of computing power contributed.

Section 2: From Concept to Reality

Chapter 5: Blockchain Applications

When looking at the application of Blockchain several things must be noted:

Firstly, Blockchain and cryptocurrencies are separate. There are many ways in which Blockchain can be applied that differ, and this is exactly the case with cryptocurrencies.

Secondly, Blockchain is a ledger and as such can have differing protocols. It is only the key traits and components that stay constant. A lot of the newer and innovative forms of Blockchain technology have their own protocols or algorithms, but they are still in the early stages of development and exist as a proof-of-concept, or as a theory.

Thirdly, the technology or platform behind the Blockchain can differ. Bitcoin is the most common platform, with most applications using a variation of that platform. However, there are many other developed platforms that can be used, each with a different protocol. These platforms each have their own strengths and drawbacks that should be considered when choosing a platform to develop a Blockchain product.

Sidechains

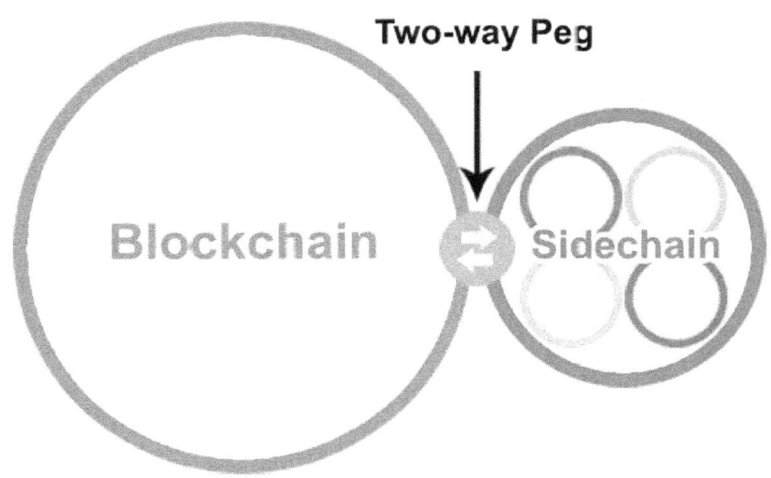

Image 03: Sidechains

Sidechains developed due to the inefficiencies of the Bitcoin Blockchain; it is not very flexible and takes a long time to adjust and make changes. Due to the size of the database that needs to be distributed with every transaction, linking the blocks has become more and more time consuming.

Sidechains are a mechanism that allows the use of a Blockchain in a separate Blockchain, think of it like a clone. The Sidechains run in parallel to the main Blockchain, and therefore Sidechains are able to be moved back to the original chain and integrated, if desired.

Because they are a Blockchain on their own that originated from another Blockchain, Sidechains possess the same traits as any other Blockchain. They also require miners to solve the puzzles and provide a proof of work. They also allow developers to experiment and develop the technology without the risk of affecting the main Blockchain.

It is this safe, contained environment that allows developers to innovate and experiment, which will provide new opportunities for applications and insights into the Blockchain. It is through this experimentation that Blockchain technology can be advanced.

Sidechains may also be more efficient at processing transaction, and may allow for the main currency to be exchanged for other cryptocurrencies. In the Bitcoin Blockchain, it is possible to split into a Sidechain and then merge back to the main Blockchain using a two-way-peg. This allows for assets to be interchangeable within the main Blockchain and the Sidechain, at a predetermined exchange rate. Therefore the Bitcoins within the Sidechain do not disappear from the system.

The implications for this in business is the possibility of "cloning" any system in place (with the appropriate licenses or permission of course), and repurposing it for the use of your own business. This can be done without affecting the original Blockchain, and operate in a new and separate environment from the original. The two-way-pegs inherent in Sidechains will also allow for the chaining of two or more of such Sidechains, opening up the possibilities of collaboration.

Blockchain in Business

The use of Blockchain is not limited to cryptocurrencies; while the original reason for Blockchain was to transfer money, recent developments have expanded the use of the technology.

Termed as "Blockchain 2.0", it is a mechanism that allows programmable transactions which can be modified based upon a set of conditions. This can be used for a variety of functions from microtransactions, to smart contracts, and the management of digital assets. It is because of this that Blockchain 2.0 is gaining popularity with companies. The business application possibilities seem limitless.

As Blockchain removes the middleman from a transaction, as in the case of cryptocurrency, this offers opportunities for businesses to improve the efficiency of transactions. By making Blockchain the middleman, an exchange can be set up between two parties. Blockchain can accomplish for free what businesses pay for, and at a much faster rate. Lowering the cost of transactions allow for businesses to be more competitive in their pricing. There are companies that have reduced processing time from several days to just hours by cutting out the middleman; as there is one less step in the process it is able to be completed much faster.

Blockchain can also be used to create smart contracts between vendors and buyers, businesses and their customers, and any two parties in the transaction chain whether it is business to business, or business to consumer.

This can be done using existing Blockchain technology, and can be implemented rather straightforwardly as compared to developing your own Blockchain. These smart contract solutions offer assurance that the transactions are legitimate, and removes any ambiguity on the terms. As Blockchain data is almost impossible to tamper with, it removes any distrust between parties as neither side is able to deny the validity of the contract. The threat of losing transaction data is also eliminated because transactions are stored in blocks across all the nodes of the network.

As with any new technology there are inherent risks, but with technology continually advancing these risks will be minimized and can be mitigated. Blockchain and smart contracts are an opportunity to solve existing issues faced by almost every business, and using them could be the advantage your business needs to get an advantage over a competitor.

It is very likely that new businesses will evolve to provide products and services to create and trade assets, track provenance, manage supply chain, manage identity, and provide ancillary services to existing industries and we will explore some of these use cases in Chapter 7.

Considerations when Implementing Blockchain

When implementing Blockchain, there are a few common considerations:

Firstly, identify innovative opportunities. Find processes that can be moved to the Blockchain. These are commonly databases, which can include customer or client data, transaction history, or any industry specific data. Blockchain technology can be used in place of database management software.

Secondly, consider the impact of the migration to Blockchain. Explore the areas where a Blockchain can add value, but yet remain in line with the strategic goals of the company. The pros and cons should be weighed at this stage, to gain a better understanding of how and why the company would use Blockchain technology.

Thirdly, consider the feasibility of the venture as well as the impact on existing systems. After understanding where Blockchain can be applied, it is important to check the feasibility of how the company wishes to implement it. This will have an effect on existing systems without a doubt.

Fourth, consider how the change process would be managed. As with the implementation of any new system, processes will need to be changed and new tools will need to be adopted. Managing the transition properly will improve the likelihood that the new systems in place will be adopted and integrated well with the rest of the business.

Chapter 6: Challenges of Implementation

While Blockchain today holds unlimited potential and there is a lot of excitement about its future, there is also an equal number of skeptics and detractors. There are challenges in implementing Blockchain technically, business-wise, and regulation-wise. In this chapter we will explore these challenges.

Technical Challenges

The main challenge with Blockchain technically is the newness of the technology, relative to existing alternatives. As Blockchain is a relatively recent technology and it is only recently being accepted in a mainstream way, the infrastructure and support are not as widespread as other technologies like mobile platforms for example.

This all boils down to the fact that there is a lack of applications available, as well as a lack of experience and understanding of what Blockchain can do, or how to apply it. However, this is the norm for new technologies especially one as disruptive as Blockchain which requires a fundamental change to the way things are currently done. Experts have compared this to the time when the Internet was just gaining traction; people are still "feeling their way" around the technology and coders are still trying to understand it. Understanding when it happens, will be exponential and once the technology takes root it will happen at a rapid pace similar to the early 2000's of the Internet. All it took then for the internet to boom was having a web browser easily available to the mass market.

Before we get there however, we will have to agree on the standard protocols. Standards can help share knowledge and make it easier to integrate and develop applications for Blockchain. The standards established would then be spurring the growth of developer kits and tools. It is not inconceivable to see turnkey solutions to deploy Blockchain technology eventually, but we will need to overcome these technical challenges before we get there.

Also, knowledge on Blockchain, including public and private keys, and smart contracts need to be better understood. Right now programmers and coders are still learning to grasp this technology, its differences from traditional databases and form use cases for Blockchain.

Business Challenges

Business challenges for Blockchain are at the macro level and affect the entire market.

Top of the list is the acceptance and value of cryptocurrencies such as Bitcoin. Volatility of these coins are still high, with Bitcoin hitting a high of almost US$20,000 in 2017 while starting the year at just under US$1,000. Market perception is the main cause; with bad press and government skepticism it is no wonder that the public are hesitant to adopt cryptocurrencies in a widespread way.

At the organization level, the issues are no less confounding. According to the University of Munich, venture capitalists have funded over one and a half billion dollars in startups in the financial, information, insurance, and communication services. However, due to the technical challenges inherent in Blockchain and the low success rate of startups, it will be some time before these startups go into the black and turn profitable.

When a successful model for Blockchain appears with a killer-app, market adoption will start to increase. Till date, there is no company that has displayed a dominance on the application of Blockchain the way Google cornered the market for internet search, or Amazon claimed the books market.

While the technology itself is mostly free and open source, there is still manpower, overheads, and other developmental costs that needs to be considered. Then there are deployment issues that need to be taken into considerations. Adopting a new technology means adopting a new mindset and a new process. Change management is a painful process as anyone who has tried to switch systems would know, and companies who adopt new technologies have to be confident of the returns in order to decide on taking the plunge. It is not uncommon for companies in a change management process to experience a loss in efficiency or suffer a loss in the short term during this period.

Business executives have to be willing to suffer this short term setback to reap the potential long term gains of implementing Blockchain.

Regulation Challenges

Some governments have reacted to cryptocurrencies negatively with cryptocurrency exchanges being shut down in Korea and China in early 2018, furthermore a number of countries have declared Bitcoin as illegal over the years.

This discomfort with cryptocurrencies from governments are due to the fact that:

- it is a currency that is not backed by a country's government or bank
- cryptocurrencies provide a layer of anonymity which may facilitate money laundering

The stance of these governments will eventually filter down the market, to policy makers, and to law enforcement agencies. Ultimately this will affect business executives, which will influence the acceptance of Blockchain.

As Blockchain is commonly associated with Bitcoin and other cryptocurrencies, regulation is likely to affect the banks and finance sectors first. Compliance and reporting may be an issue for these institutions as they adopt Blockchain technology, and it would be a step back for the technology if an entire industry were to hesitate adoption or dismiss the technology altogether.

Another concern with governments is the jurisdiction of Blockchains. As nodes are located in separate locations, it is possible and even likely for some of these nodes to be located out of the country. If a fault were to occur in a contract or should a dispute arise, it would be difficult to enforce a contract as it is not clear which government or set of laws would have jurisdiction.

In the case of Blockchain being used for trade, liability is the least of a government's worries. The inability to control or stop certain transactions also means a potential loss in tax revenue, and also means that some policies like protectionism, levies, or bans are less effective. When trade data is made private on a Blockchain, it becomes easier to hide such transactions to evade tax, or circumvent any trade protection policies in place.

Chapter 7: Using Blockchain Technology

Blockchain Use in Monetary Administration

Trade Processing

In conventional trade processing, individual ledgers are maintained by each firm, and are reconciled regularly. Having a Blockchain ledger replaces these individual ledger with a single ledger managed by all the firms on the Blockchain network. This speeds up the regulatory reporting as the data is centrally stored, and fraud can be reduced because transaction data cannot be altered once part of the Blockchain.

Such a system processes data in real time, as manpower is no longer needed to authenticate and very each trade as it happens; instead automation built into the system can take over. This reduces errors in the processing, and improves the efficiency of the process. By eliminating the requirement of a middleman, the procedure is also streamlined.

Preparing Insurance Claims

Blockchain, as applied to handling insurance claims, is reinventing the claims handling process. When there is a Blockchain network, claims are able to be processed in a more timely, transparent, and objective manner. By using smart contracts with data analysis, it is possible to automatically run through the insurance assessment criteria. Smart contracts can be used to define the objective criteria that come into play in an insurance policy, and thus reduce the scope of any disputes.

As with trade processing, the benefits of this are a reduction in errors, an improvement in the efficiency of the process, a reduction of errors, and additionally fraud prevention.

International Payments

Blockchain is being used in the area of international or cross-border payments, the cryptocurrency Ripple, is quite likely to make international or cross-border transfers free, but that is not all. Ripple is intended to act as a bridge currency to other currencies, enabling businesses to register and open a "gateway" and act as a credit intermediary.

Additionally, bank accounts powered by cryptocurrencies are now appearing in the finance industry. Using Blockchain technology to record banking transactions in a ledger ensures that the transactions recorded are tamper proof, and provide a higher level of security between the banking institutions and their customers. This allows banks who share the same Blockchain network to transfer money between account holders in a much more efficient way.

Syndicated Lending

Blockchain has been used to develop a platform for syndicated loans. In this use case, Blockchain drives transparency and efficiency by improving the data sharing between the lenders and borrowers. Real time transactions data, balances, and other information can be accessed by anyone on the platform which improves the decision making through automation and perfect sharing of information.

Blockchain Use in Property Transactions

Title Management

Managing property titles is challenging due to high costs associated with fraud prevention, risk mitigation, and due diligence among others. Using Blockchain it is possible to give each property its own digital identity, including purchase history, location, and other details on the title.

Being tamper proof means that it is difficult to commit fraud related to rights, transfer, or other details. Having this information on a Blockchain network increases the trust and proficiency of real estate management companies.

Due Diligence and Financial Evaluation

Blockchain is being used to assist in due diligence activities when purchasing property. The data on each property can be assigned to a Blockchain to expedite the pre-transaction process which is expensive and time consuming. This includes financial, environmental, and legal challenges, and the costs of such are usually factored into the sale. This process when done manually is also subject to errors.

Other Uses of Blockchain

Internet of Things

The Internet of Things (IOT) is basically a perpetually online device that is gathering data in our everyday lives. Together with Blockchain it becomes a secure and permanent method of recording the data collected by these devices.

This provides transparency into their use: activities can be analyzed and tracked by anyone connected to the network. The application of this is in tracking sensors or authentication of trusted users.

IBM released a report in early 2018 categorizing the use of Blockchain in IOT to three areas:

1. **Device Identity**

   This is a secure way to authenticate the origin of a product, or the authorization access of the person holding the device. Alternatively, it could be used to verify the origin of the device, including the source of its components.

2. **Device Transactions**

   This is a secure way to authenticate and automate the exchange and settlement of services. This can be used to pay for goods and services accessed by the user or device.

3. **Device Interactions**

   This is a secure way to centralize all interactions, evens and updates associated with the device. This could be used for diagnostics, updates, repairs, or ownership.

Healthcare

Blockchain can be used to create a record of patient information, including treatment received, medical history, and timestamps to verify the diagnosis. As the current healthcare system is fragmented and are not well designed to manage the volume and detail of data that is being produced, this is an opportunity of Blockchain to be adopted.

The use of a universal ledger would see patient information being readily accessible and up to date, and can be used to provide a higher level of care. Switching doctors or insurance companies would be less of a hassle with patient records stored on the Blockchain.

Chapter 8: Real World Examples

Blockchain Consortiums

Since Blockchain is a technology that requires a network, naturally organizations will banded together to create consortiums to collaborate. As of the end of 2017, there were slightly over 40 consortiums that have been formed globally, with approximately 60% in the financial sector. However, there are other industries such as healthcare and logistics that are forming a consortium as well, and the trend is showing that they are gaining in acceptance.

Consortiums are a means for companies to work together to solve business problems by forming an association. These consortiums benefit their members with sharing of credit information between banks, or facilitating trade or cross border monetary transfers by pooling their resources together.

Collaborative efforts between industries are also taking shape, with companies from different industries gathering together to develop Blockchain Platforms that can be repurposed based on technical standards. Hyperledger and the Enterprise Ethereum Alliance are examples of such platforms.

Enterprise Ethereum Alliance

The Enterprise Ethereum Alliance (EEA), started in 2016, and is registered as a non-profit corporation, whose mission is to "evolve Ethereum into an enterprise-grade technology"

The EEA develops provides best practices, open standards, open-source references, and tools to enable Ethereum to be used by enterprises in various industries, taking into consideration the complexities and differences between them.

This consortium works as an open-source Blockchain initiative that connects Fortune 500 enterprises, startups, and academics. Among its members are several powerhouses such as Cisco, Microsoft, IBM, Intel, CME Group, J.P. Morgan, and BNY Mellon.

There are several working groups under the EEA created by members based upon their needs and business opportunities. Each group is focused on a specific industry such as "Advertising" or "Insurance", or tasked to face a specific challenge such as "Integration and Tools" or "Communications Protocols". Members are encouraged to join these working groups based upon their expertise.

Hyperledger

Hyperledger is an open source collaborate effort aimed to develop cross-industry Blockchain technology for enterprise use. The difference between Hyperledger and the Ethereum Enterprise Association is their approach to design and their target audience. Hyperledger was designed with more flexibility in mind to cater to the customization needs of different organizations, while the EEA is focused more on public networks and smart contracts.

Hyperledger is hosted by the Linux Foundation and focuses on Blockchain technologies instead of any specific cryptocurrencies. Their membership counts over 120 member organizations, including Accenture, American Express, and Cisco, IBM, and SAP.

The goal of Hyperledger is to advance Blockchain technologies and promote commercial adoption through transparency, longevity, interoperability and support. This is done through the allocation of code, funding, and/or resources to the benefit of Hyperledger's community-sourced projects.

They are working on 9 projects at the moment from developing foundational Blockchain, to developing toolkits, and building a modular approach to Blockchain.

R3

R3 started as a company founded to work on tackling inefficiencies in the finance sector. They have since grown into an open source Blockchain project designed for businesses.

The main purpose of their project known as Corda, is to record, manage, and reconcile financial transactions and agreements between banks and financial institutions. However, unlike a standard Blockchain, Corda only shares data with parties that have a legitimate need to know. It achieves this by facilitating the workflow between companies and achieves a consensus for each individual transaction and then records a link between a contract document and smart contract code.

CULedger

Once known as CUBlockchain, CULedger was formed by a group of credit unions and service providers in 2017. It's aim was to develop and create a private, permissioned distributed shared ledger for credit unions. With membership numbers around 60, including 3rd party technology firms and associations from the United States, Europe, and Canada they are not as large as the EEA or Hyperledger, but rather are focused on a specific use case in the financial sector.

In February 2018, they released a digital ledger based identity system intended for use by credit unions to prevent identity theft and fraud. By using the peer to peer network, users' records are secure and they only share as much information as is required for transactions.

Other Real World Examples of Blockchain in Business

As Blockchain has been around for almost 10 years, there are already companies that are using this technology as a part of their business. The Technical University of Munich published a research paper on Blockchain and how it has disrupted or may disrupt various industries. Most of the startups can be found in Canada, the United States, and the United Kingdom. In addition, there are also established multinationals and governments who have implemented Blockchain technology in their operations.

Here are a few examples of real world applications of Blockchain:

Case 1: Barclays Bank

Barclays have implemented Blockchain in identity verification, and in trade finance hence there are two use cases here grouped in this case.

Company Background: Barclays is a British multinational bank and financial services company that was founded in 1690. They are headquartered in London.

How they used Blockchain: Barclays have used Blockchain to eliminate identity theft. Background checks for new staff and customers can take weeks but with Blockchain, it is possible to check an identity against sanctions lists, law enforcement databases, past financial records and other databases.

Benefits: Through the use of Blockchain Barclays has shortened the process for verifying and understanding the identities and histories of their staff (for screening) and customers (for customer relations).

How they used Blockchain: Barclays have also used Blockchain in trade finance. Traditionally, a bill of lading is required to endorse a transaction between buyers and sellers. By using a platform called Wave, the bank can securely sign, endorse, and transfer bill of ladings alongside other documents in a transaction.

Benefits: Through the use of Blockchain Barclays has shortened the process for completing a global transaction from up to twenty days to a matter of hours.

Case 2: Gem

Company Background: Gem is a new started based in California, they are slated for a launch in mid 2018. They originated as a pilot project from MIT.

How they used Blockchain: Currently medical records are stored in many incompatible backend systems and data on patients is incomplete or outdated. Gem uses a Blockchain application for storing electronic medical records.

With Blockchain technology, Gem is creating a ledger with the records of patients to decenralize the management of healthcare data.

Benefits: Still a work in progress, but it is intended that when live, it would be used with the Center for Disease Control (CDC) to manage outbreaks and medical relief.

Case 3: Loyyal

Company Background: Loyyal was founded in 2014, and is headquartered in San Francisco.

How they used Blockchain: Loyyal provides a loyalty platform utilizing Blockchain and smart contract technology. This platform includes the tools to deploy and manage aand support dynamic and unique reward models.

Benefits: Loyyal introduces interoperability to the currently fragmented loyalty rewards industry. This includes multi-branded coalitions, superior program liability management and dynamic issuance and redemption options customized for each unique relationship. All these are made possible with Blockchain.

Case 4: REMME

Company Background: REMME started in 2015. While they did not provide an address, they have a strong web presence on various social media and engage with their customers and followers.

How they used Blockchain: This company provides security to existing critical infrastructure. REMME uses a decentralized authentication system in place of passwords and user IDs. Instead, SSL certificates stored on a Blockchain are used to login to systems.

Benefits: REMME builds a high end secure system with a distributed Public Key Infrastructure to enhance security in their client's systems.

Case 5: SKUChain

Company Background: SKUChain is a Californian startup founded in 2014.

How they used Blockchain: This company uses Blockchain to empower enterprise supply chains. Blockchain is used to provide transparency, security, and efficiency to the supply chain.

Benefits: SKUChain allows users to understand the history of the products uploaded to the Blockchain. This enables enterprise customers to plan and collaborate with each other while keeping sensitive information confidential.

Companies on SKUChain's platform are also able to engage with customers enabling one-to-one marketing.

Conclusion

Thank you for taking the time to read this book!

After reading this book, you would have a better understanding of the possibilities brought about by Blockchain; what it is, what its benefits are, and how it is being used in different industries.

Implementing Blockchain is not without its challenges and uncertainties, however there are opportunities and rewards for those willing to risk and develop competency in this emerging field. Without these pioneers, we would certainly not be reaping the benefits Blockchain could bring us.

Blockchain is a lot more than cryptocurrencies, and a lot more than a business tool. If harnessed properly, I believe that it is a technology that would create changes in our world that will last for decades to come.

If you enjoyed this book, please take the time to leave me a review on Amazon. I appreciate your honest feedback, and it really helps me to continue producing high quality books.

This is the 6 x 9 Basic Template. Paste your manuscript into this template or simply start typing. Delete this text prior to use.

7

www.ingramcontent.com/pod-product-compliance
Lightning Source LLC
Chambersburg PA
CBHW070419230526
45471CB00006B/2879